# A Nature Walk on the Farm

Louise and Richard Spilsbury

Raintree

Raintree is an imprint of Capstone Global Library Limited, a company incorporated in England and Wales having its registered office at 7 Pilgrim Street, London, EC4V 6LB – Registered company number: 6695582

www.raintreepublishers.co.uk
myorders@raintreepublishers.co.uk

Edited by Joanna Issa, Penny West, Krissy Mohn, and Gina Kammer
Designed by Cynthia Akiyoshi
Picture research by Elizabeth Alexander and Tracy Cummins
Production by Helen McCreath
Originated by Capstone Global Library Ltd
Printed and bound in China by Leo Paper Group

ISBN 978 1 406 28218 4
18  17  16  15  14
10 9 8 7 6 5 4 3 2 1

**British Library Cataloguing in Publication Data**
A full catalogue record for this book is available from the British Library.

**Acknowledgements**
We would like to thank the following for permission to reproduce photographs:

Alamy: © deadgooddesigns, 21, © Design Pics Inc., 18, © Nigel Cattlin, 19; FLPA: © John Eveson, 17, © Nigel Cattlin, 13, © Wayne Hutchinson, 5; Getty Images: Dorling Kindersley/Gary Ombler, 16, Ned Frisk, 20; naturepl.com, © Andy Rouse, 15, © Philippe Clement, 14; Shutterstock, 1000 Words, 11, back cover, Acon Cheng, 8, adiia Korol, 22 top left, Anettphoto, 6, back cover left, Binkski, design element (fence), bjonesphotography, front cover, back cover right, DenisNata, design element (grass), Dieter H, 12, Dionisvera, design element (pea), Eric Gevaert, front cover, Eric Isselee, design element (owl), (pig), (sheep), Hintau Aliaksei, design element (frog), illustrart, design element (wheat), irin-k, design element (bee), Khomulo Anna , design element (wildflowers), Lepas, design element (duck), Ikordela, 9, Oleksiy Mark, bottom left, Pavel Vakhrushev, design element (blue flowers), (red flowers), romrf, 22 bottom right, Ruud Morijn Photographer, 10, spirit of america, 4, T Cassidy, 22 top right, Tatiana Volgutova, 7

We would like to thank Michael Bright for his invaluable help in the preparation of this book.

# Contents

Some words are shown in bold, **like this**. You can find out what they mean by looking in the glossary.

# Where are we going?

We are going on a nature walk to spot plants and animals on a farm. Some farms grow **crops**, which are plants that people eat. Some farms keep animals that we use for food. Some do both!

First get permission to visit a farm. Farms can
be muddy, so wear rubber boots. It is best not
to touch the animals, and you should wash
your hands after your walk.

# What grows in the field?

Can you see the **grain** growing at the top of these tall, grass-like plants? These are wheat plants. People crush and grind the grain to make flour for bread and pasta.

6

Look at the shapes inside the green **pods**. These are pea plants, and the round, green peas growing inside the pods are nice to eat.

# What lives on the flowers?

Use a magnifying glass to spot **insects** on farm flowers. Look in the centre of the flowers. Many insects come to drink a sugary juice called **nectar** from here.

Bees lick up nectar with their long tongues. Some bees have yellow and black stripes on their bodies, which warn animals they can give a nasty sting.

# What is behind the fence?

Look at the tuft of white fur on the fence.
What do you think lives behind the fence?
The grass in the field should give you a clue.

Sheep have thick hair called wool that sometimes rubs off on fences. They eat tough grass plants. Their big, hard, front teeth cut through the grass, and the flat, back teeth grind it up.

# What happens in the hen house?

Peep into the hen house to see lots of busy hens. Hens lay eggs inside a hen house. The hen house protects the hens from foxes that might try to eat them.

Hens lay eggs to have young, but farm eggs do not have **chicks** inside. When the farmer takes the eggs away to eat or sell, the hens keep laying more.

# What lives in the barn?

Look on the floor for clues about what lives up high in a barn. These pellets contain hair and bone from small animals. What do you think made them?

Barn owls rest in the barn in the day. They hunt mice and other small animals at night. They swallow **prey** whole and cough up the animal bones and hair in pellets later.

# What lives in the mud?

What do you see in this muddy field? What animal do you think made those shapes and holes in the mud? Why do you think it made them?

Pigs roll in mud to keep cool. Being muddy also protects them from biting **insects** and sunburn. Pigs root around in the mud to get insects and worms to eat too.

# What is in the pond?

Cows, sheep, and other animals drink from the pond. Why do you think this duck is upside down in the pond? Ducks feed on plants, **insects**, and small fish that are under the water.

Can you see the eggs in this pond? The **tadpoles** swimming out of the eggs live underwater. Later they will grow legs and become frogs living on the land.

19

# How can I protect farm animals and plants?

You can help to protect farm animals and plants by staying on paths, so you do not step on **crops**. Keep dogs on leads too, so they do not chase farm animals.

Leave gates on a farm as you found them.
A farmer usually closes gates to keep
farm animals in. But, they may be open so
animals can reach food and water.

# Exploring nature

These things will help you explore farms on a nature walk.

notepad

binoculars

pencil

nature spotter's guide

magnifying glass

# Glossary

**chick** baby bird

**crop** plant that farmers grow for people to eat or use to make food

**grain** the seeds on a cereal plant such as wheat, rice, corn, rye, or barley

**insect** small animal that has six legs when it is an adult

**nectar** sweet juice in the centre of a flower

**pod** container or case that holds plant seeds such as peas

**prey** type of animal that is eaten by other animals

**tadpole** baby frog

# Find out more

## Books

*Farming* (The Geography Detective Investigates), Jen Green (Wayland, 2013)

*Farm* (Scholastic Discover More), Penny Arlon (Scholastic, 2012)

## Websites

**http://kids.nationalgeographic.com/kids/photos/gallery/farm-animals/**
Check out cool facts and photos of farm animals.

**http://www.animalcorner.co.uk/farm/farm.html**
Learn more about animals that live on farms.

# Index